MARGIE:
My Life with Bipolar

by Margaret A. Graham

DORRANCE
PUBLISHING CO
EST. 1920
PITTSBURGH, PENNSYLVANIA 15238

Dorrance Publishing Co
585 Alpha Drive
Pittsburgh, PA 15238
Visit our website at *www.dorrancebookstore.com*

ISBN: 979-8-8852-7103-5
ISBN: 979-8-8852-7830-0

MARGIE:
My Life with Bipolar

Introduction

"I can do all things through Christ who strengthens me"

Philippians 4:13

I am a woman who was diagnosed with a mental illness called manic depressive illness in 1980 at age 25. It is now called bipolar. It is a psychiatric illness characterized by both manic and depressive mood swings.

I have written my memoir relating my life from childhood to present day being afflicted with an affective disorder.

I dedicate this memoir to all the people, friends and family, who prayed for me while I was ill and who continue to keep me in prayer to this day.

Early Childhood

MY MEMORY GOES BACK TO AGE THREE OR FOUR. I ALWAYS FELT I was different from other children. I was in touch with my emotions and feelings at a very young age. I think having an affective disorder was the reason. Another characteristic I had as well was being sensitive to other people's emotions. Even on one occasion when I was being disciplined by my father I recall him saying to me, "You are different than all the other kids." I was stunned and felt betrayed. I have never forgotten that moment. My dad also used to say, "Will you ever amount to much?" This did not help my already shy personality and low self-esteem. Throughout much of my childhood I was afraid of him. As he aged, however, and I became an adult, he exhibited a more loving personality. As a child, though, he was not very loving towards me. My behavior could send him into a rage. I could not always count on my mother to rescue me from these escapades. Occasionally she would say, "Leon, you are frightening her." She was right. When Dad was angry, fire seemed to come out of his eyes. He looked wild. Needless to say, both parents were inconsistent with their expression of love for me. My childhood lacked the loving, nurturing, attentiveness that a shy, affective disordered child needs and strives for. I needed reassurance and security. There was neither praise nor positive affirmations. I have no recollection of a display of affection towards me through hugs and kisses. Fear was the main emotion that ran parallel with my childhood: fear of punishment, fear of divorce, and fear of shame if other people found out what went on behind our closed doors.

I was the fourth of sixth children, ranging in age from one to eighteen years. My birthday is 12/12/1954. I was baptized, Catholic but I am not certain of the actual date. I believe it was during the Christmas season, because I found a picture of my parents holding a baby in front of a Christmas tree. I was named Margaret Ann Fanslow. My mother wanted me to be called Margaret Ann, but a priest friend of the family nicknamed me Margie and the name stuck.

Later in my adult life, I realized that December 12th is the feast of our Lady of Guadalupe, the Patroness of the Americas. I've always had a great devotion to Our Lady and felt very privileged to share my birthday with her feast day and to have her as my patron saint.

When I was about four, we got a male Collie dog, which we named Laddie. He grew to be a big dog and I was very little. He would jump up on me, being taller than me. This behavior was intimidating to me. Also, he was a runner, and chased cars and motorcycles. Although our backyard was fenced, he would get out and be off and running. It was not long before my parents were sick of this situation. So it was decided that he should go to my mother's niece and her family who lived on a farm. I remember this being a sad day since I had gotten attached to him. And to make matters worse, when we went to visit him, he was not there. They said he just ran away and never came back. I was broken-hearted. That was the only pet we ever had as I grew up.

I recall an incident when I could have been as young as three or four. My brother, Bob (who is just 14 months older), and I were playing outside. I had the great idea to go for a walk to the Thunder Bay River, which was about a block and a half away from our house. So off we went. When we arrived at the riverbank behind the paper mill where my godfather, Uncle Eddie, worked, he spotted us. Of course, he took us home, when he saw we were in danger of falling in and drowning. Well, my parents scolded both of us, but Bobby got the spanking because he was older and should have known better. I felt so sorry for him because I knew it was all my idea.

My mother planned a surprise birthday party when I turned five. We had a recreation room in the basement which I helped decorate for the party which was to be the following day. Then my dad took me for an errand. When we returned my mother called me to come downstairs. That's when everybody yelled, "Surprise!" I truly was elated. We had a fun time playing pin the tail on the donkey, musical chairs, and drop the clothes pin into the bottle. We enjoyed the cake and ice cream, too. This is an example of one of my mother's better times. It was an expression of her love for me and a fond memory.

In kindergarten, I was shy, quiet, and apprehensive around people. As I would walk the five blocks to the public school, I often met up with a group of rowdy kids who frightened me. Frequently, I would turn around and return home to get a ride from my father. Occasionally, I met up with a tiny blonde-haired, blue-eyed, cute girl and we walked the last two blocks together. I was always glad when that happened. However, we were in different classes, which disappointed me.

In kindergarten, we had nap time on our foam mats. One day I opened my eyes to peak and the teacher, Mrs. Werder, tapped me on the foot with a yard stick and told me to shut my eyes and rest. I was so afraid she would call my mother, but to my relief, she didn't. I never peaked again!

I attended St. Mary Catholic School from grades one through eight, and was taught by nuns of the Felician order. My mother sewed a very cute red corduroy jumper for my first day. She was an expert seamstress. With a white blouse underneath it, I was as proud as a peacock. However, **she, like most mothers did,** would not take me to school. She insisted that my dad take me and drop me off at the classroom. I was disappointed.

First grade was quite uneventful, although my desk partner was a girl who never talked. This was frustrating to me because neither I nor the teacher could get her to speak.

I developed a crush on a boy named Jay that year and I let him know it. He in turn told me he liked someone else. That was the beginning of many of my school year crushes. I did not know then but have learned later that people with bipolar disorder have a strong need to be in a relationship with the opposite sex.

Throughout my school years, I always had a best girlfriend. My mother would occasionally allow me to have sleepovers and a few slumber parties. I was somewhat reluctant to sleep at other friend's homes because I was a bed wetter. This was traumatic. At home, Dad would usually come and help me change during the night and put towels down on the wet sheets. This was an example of his compassion.

In second grade, I caught on to the fact that I was quite bright. I was elected class president, and when Sister Roberta had to leave the room, it was my duty to take over the lesson she was teaching. I would march up in front of the class and act just like the teacher. On one occasion, I could see Sister eavesdropping on me as she visited with the teacher next door. I felt proud of my performance. School is where I achieved and got my affirmations. At home, I lacked the attention that a child needs who has the predisposition to a mental illness.

I still remember my first Confession and how I told the priest that I had disobeyed my parents a million times! This is just an example of my poor self-esteem at home. I cried often during those impressionable years. One memory I have never forgotten is this: I prayed silently to Jesus, "Why couldn't I have been your mother?" If I were Jesus' mother, I knew I would be happy.

I made my First Holy Communion on May 19, 1963 and it was the highlight of my life thus far! I have truly fond memories of receiving this sacrament and I felt so close to Jesus. It was a profoundly inspirational experience. I also recall looking in the mirror and thinking how beautiful I looked in my lacy white dress, and the long, curled, dark brown locks that my mother had done to fix my hair. I believed I was truly ready to receive this sacrament.

In second grade, I started to eat compulsively. Some of the foods were donuts, fudge, and ice cream. I remember stopping at a relative's bakery on the way to school for a hot donut free of charge. It was delicious. I had a predisposition to this disorder. I even remember both my teacher and my father commenting that I was getting chubby. I wasn't aware at that time that I was gaining weight.

Also, in second and third grade, I belonged to the Brownie Troop. I was elected the scribe for two years. I had to write an article of what we did each week and deliver it to the local Alpena News office before the deadline of printing. I did not cherish this role, as I had to walk downtown, almost a mile away by myself.

I recall most of my teachers' names in grade school. Sr. Jacinta in first grade, Sr. Roberta in second grade, Miss Connor in third grade, Mrs. Murray in fourth, Sr. Angelita in fifth, Sr. Frumentia or Pious in sixth, no memory of seventh grade, and Sr. Maximillian in eighth.

The nuns, for the most part, were kind and gentle. I was an A-B student and my grades were important. In fifth grade, we had an exam which was to be our grade on our report card. I received a D on it. Sr. Angelita saw how devastated I was. She took me outside of the classroom into the hallway. She told me I could get a C for my final grade…I was grateful to her.

I do recall a different elderly nun who humiliated me when I was in sixth grade. There was some commotion near the area where I sat. I was not even involved. However, she called me out and asked me my last name. "How can you behave like that being a Fanslow?" she exclaimed. There was no standing up for oneself so I just took the abuse.

My oldest brother, Ron, went to the seminary when I was eight. The first Sunday of the month was family visiting day. Mom never missed this day. We all piled into our station wagon for the four-hour drive to Ann Arbor, Michigan. I was always relegated to the area without seats, which was an awful experience. It was a long ride in an uncomfortable position.

My baby sister, Paula, was born the summer before third grade. I was like a mother to her. I would feed her a noon bottle and rock her to sleep before putting her down in the crib for a nap. As she grew, I could sense she was special to my mother who was now 42 years old. This child got the attention that I craved but lacked. She grew to be a very outgoing little girl, never shy like me. At times I resented her for her positive characteristics.

I was confirmed in sixth grade and chose my confirmation name as St. Therese of Lisieux. This name was a direct order from my mother. Ever since then, I've had a devotion to The Little Flower, as she was also known. During this service I recalled a thought, "Remember this day." My confirmation sponsor was a second cousin who was around my mother's age.

I recall in grade school my parents never attending parent-teacher night. The following day, our teacher had all the children raise their hand if their parent's had attended. I was always embarrassed when I could not raise my hand.

I wanted to take dance lessons but was not given that opportunity. I wanted to join the Girl's Club. Finally, I convinced my mother to register me. After that, I was on my own. The walk to the club was about a mile away. I had to go across an old covered bridge with a very narrow sidewalk. That was very frightening. Needless to say, I only went there a few times.

I was enrolled in swim class, but after the first day, was on my own as well. The pool was located in the big old high school. Going there alone was a frightening and terrifying experience. After being made to jump into the deep end of the pool and thinking I would drown, I quit going to those lessons, too. I had little encouragement and support in those endeavors. I received no moral support from either parent.

There was a library downtown that I was not even aware existed. One time I went there with a friend and was in awe of all the books. My parents never took me to the library or encouraged me to read.

In sixth grade, I began going through puberty and realized I was fat. I was bigger than my mother who weighed 125 pounds, and my older sister, Mary Ellen, whose clothes I would sometimes borrow. This prompted my first of many diets. I had an appendectomy as a result of the dieting and lost lots of weight. I remember the scale reading 99 lbs. in the hospital before I was discharged. I was elated! When I went back to school all the kids commented on how much weight I had lost. The funny thing was I never thought my classmates saw me as fat. My excess weight did not seem to affect me emotionally even though I wore chubby girl clothes. I was never bullied due to my size.

At one sleepover party, we were caught smoking cigarettes. We were all terrified that Debbie's mom would call each of our mom's, but through the grace of God, she didn't. What a relief!

Although we lived just blocks from the beaches of Lake Huron, my parents never took us there. By sixth grade, I was able to walk or ride my bike to a friend's house. She lived right around the corner from Thompson Beach Park. We would go to the beach and cool off in the chilly water. The big lake never warmed up completely but it was refreshing and fun once you got used to the temperature. With friends whose families had boats, I learned to water ski. Those were fun days of which memories I cherish.

For the most part our Christmases were full of good memories. We each received a few things we had requested. We were not wealthy so we were never spoiled with many gifts.

I recall searching for the hidden unwrapped presents throughout the closets, cubby holes, and the basement fruit cellar. Sometimes I found them and other times they were stored at an aunt and uncles, or my grandparents'. I remember one Christmas Eve being sneaky and gently un-taping a present to find a beautiful yellow sweater. Another year as a youngster, I remember counting the number of gifts each child was to receive. I had the least and felt bad about that. My mother quickly went to the nearest drug store and bought several items to make things look more even to me. She was kind on those occasions. Mom always did the Christmas shopping and often went to Saginaw or Detroit to find special items of stylish clothes. I don't recall my parents exchanging presents. However, my siblings did exchange gifts with each other.

On Christmas Eve, we often attended Midnight Mass. Then we would come home and eat French meat pie, tourtiere. It was bought and made from a secret recipe of my mother's first cousin who owned a bakery. Christmas Day, we would awake during the night to see if Santa had arrived yet. If he indeed had, we each were allowed to look at one present as Santa's gifts were never wrapped. Then we had to return to bed and wait until morning to open the rest of our gifts from each other.

On Christmas Day, various aunts and uncles and my paternal grandparents always dropped in unannounced for a drink and cookies. My mother made the best cookies: cherry winks, pecan sandies, sugar cookies, and her infamous Fantasy fudge. It was just the thing to do….go visiting. My memories of these times are mostly positive.

We always received an envelope from Grandma and Grandpa Fanslow with a 2-dollar bill in it. I do remember receiving a 2-dollar bill from my grandma after I was married in one of the letters we exchanged. She said, "See how long you can keep it!" It is still wrapped in our family Bible.

I do remember one Christmas when my mom was not feeling well and stayed on the couch the whole day. I felt sorry for her. Another characteristic I had was being sensitive to other peoples' emotions.

During most of my childhood, family life was quite dysfunctional. My mother suffered from migraine headaches, fatigue, and mood swings. She exhibited signs of a nervous ailment for as long as I can remember. She visited many doctors for these symptoms. They could find nothing wrong. Her doctor thought her condition was psychosomatic. She desperately wanted to be well but was often in bed when I returned from school. I felt sorry for her. If she was not depressed, her mood was elevated. Her health contributed to an unhealthy marriage. Our family was the brunt of her high and low mood swings.

My parents argued much of the time when her mood was escalated. At these times she would reprimand us children for any simple mistake. I do remember being slapped for no good reason at all.

Provoking my dad into quarrels would happen at these times. She would imply that he was having an affair when he never strayed from their marital vows. She would get in his face until he'd eventually shove her and a physical fight ensued. This was hard to witness as a young child. I recall fights during the night, too. Many nights I would awake to screaming, yelling, and threats of my dad leaving. One time my dad was at the door with a suitcase in hand and my brother and I were clinging to his coat begging him to stay. He never left but turned to beer to cope with such antics. If my dad's car were in the driveway when I returned from school, I knew they had had a fight after his lunch hour and there would be unrest for the rest of the evening.

Never would I bring a friend home from school unannounced. I knew that if the curtains were drawn and the doors all closed that my mother would be sick in bed with a towel tightly wrapped around her head. I could see she was in pain and knew deep in my heart she was sick. The doctors could never find anything wrong with her. They made her think it was all in her head. Years later, we found out that they were right about that. She did have an undiagnosed brain disease (manic depression), which I inherited. One brother also has bipolar illness but exhibits depression instead of manias. Other cousins suffered with mental illnesses, so it was familial.

Between the extreme highs and the extreme lows of my mother's moods, there was some normalcy in our home. Although it was rare, I did witness affection by my parents on one occasion. They exchanged an embrace and kiss, which I witnessed. The memory stuck with me and was the hope I clung to for my relationships in adult life.

At other times, Mom could be loving, kind, and generous with neighbors, family, and friends. My maternal grandmother lived with us often because she could not live on her own. My mother refused to put her in a nursing home despite the objections of her siblings.

She also donated our old clothes and toys to the poor. When she was feeling well, I often came home to the smell of freshly baked bread or chocolate chip cookies.

High School

CATHOLIC CENTRAL WAS WHERE I ENTERED HIGH SCHOOL IN ninth grade. I went from a class of 20 to a class of 100 when all of the Catholic grade schools merged. My parents were known as the Catholic radicals and were always keeping tabs on whether the dogma of the church was being taught. These were years when Catholic priests and nuns were leaving their orders for one reason or another. I felt like I was ostracized by the staff because of my parents' visibility. This did not stop me from becoming vice-president of our class. I was quite confident with all of the new students and made friends readily. I was heart-broken, though, when I didn't make the cheerleading squad. My parents gave me no sympathy. I remember sobbing until no more tears would fall from my swollen eyes.

I was a very sassy teenager and swore often at both parents during arguments with them. This behavior was learned from their example, yet I was still ashamed of it. I made weekly trips to confession to try and change this habit. I even confided in my new girlfriends from Catholic Central to ask if they treated their parents in the same manner. I was ashamed when they told me they did not talk that way to their parents. That was a wakeup call to me to change my behavior. My mother was tolerant and forgiving of my sarcastic, foul-mouthed behavior towards her during our intense disagreements.

Our high school was set to close in two years. So, in tenth grade, my best friend and I decided to go to the public school, Alpena High, and start fresh with all the incoming tenth graders. Now I was a little fish in a big pond of

500 students. I was overwhelmed with the number of students in attendance and my shyness became more overt. I didn't join any extracurricular activities. I did make a new friend on the very first day in study hall. She was really outgoing and I was in the limelight because of her.

We remained super close throughout high school, college, and as young adults. We were each other's maid-of honor at our perspective weddings.

Drinking wine and beer was the activity of choice for much of my high school years. The boys built an A-frame in the woods where we would gather, have bonfires, and drink Boones Farm and beer. We also partied at each other's houses when our parents were out of town. I recall getting sick and having hangovers on Saturday mornings. My dad would say, "That's what you get for drinking." I was never punished for this behavior. We also frequented the local bars once we were of legal age. The ones I recall are the Tap Room, the Owl, and Twin Acres.

In my teens, I had a premonition that one day I would lose my mind. It was just for a fleeting moment and I never paid it any attention but tucked it away in my memory. I believe now it was a forewarning from God.

I did inherit some of my mother's good qualities, which were to my advantage. I had dieted in sixth grade after my weight skyrocketed out of control. So now I was petite, and was attractive like her, and had her dark auburn, long curly hair with sky-blue eyes. I don't want to sound vain, but I always had a boyfriend or at least a date for every occasion. I hung with the "in crowd" and the "jocks" but always felt a little removed or not totally accepted. I also had separate friends from other cliques as well.

As I said earlier, we would often go to midnight Mass on Christmas Eve. One year when I was in high school, this boy I hardly knew called me up to see if I would go to Mass with him. The only way I knew him was because he started following me to a class I had when it was his lunch hour. We became friends but I never considered him a boyfriend. In those days, the downtown stores were open on Monday nights. Teenagers would congregate and visit and get cokes from the local dime store. One time when he was in our group I went into the most exclusive dress store in town. My mother shopped there and would once in a while allow me to purchase something for a special occasion. That time when he was in the store with me, I pulled a dress from the rack and really admired it. I said how much I liked it. Well, getting back to Christmas Eve, I did go to Mass with him but sat as close to my family as I could. When we returned home, I didn't invite him in. Then he presented me with a big box that was beautifully wrapped. I opened it reluctantly as I had no present for him nor felt I should have one. Well, in the box was that beautiful navy blue, red, and white knit dress I had admired in the store. I said I could not accept it. He insisted so I took it, thanked him, and bade him farewell.

The word got out at school about this gift. Some kids said he stole it. Others said he really did buy it. The dilemma was that the owner of the store had a daughter in my class. My mother knew the owner as she frequented the store and they lived down the street. I just could never wear the dress to school, not knowing the truth about how he obtained it. So I planned with two of my best friends to take it to his house and return it. We got to his house and they ducked down in the car as I went to the door. I gave him the box, which held the dress. He still said he bought it, but I said it was just too expensive of a gift. As we left, the three of us had a good laugh over this experience and I breathed a sigh of relief.

There were always undercurrents from my mother that I would get pregnant. I dated lots of boys from age 14 through the time I got married at 21. I did manage to remain a virgin, although I was not lily white. I just loved to play kissy-face and did tease many a date. Promiscuity is another sign of bipolar illness. I certainly knew how to attract a boy if I set out to do so.

Beginning with my freshman year in high school, I remember sleeping a lot. I did have a case of mononucleosis, but after recovering from that, I still took naps after school on a regular basis. On Sundays, I would refuse to go visiting the relatives with the family if my mom were in good spirits. I chose to stay home and spent many afternoons asleep on the couch. In retrospect these were the beginning days of my depressive state.

My parents had a strong Catholic faith. Mother had been in the convent for five years but left before taking her final vows. I believe I inherited her strong belief and faith in God, and the love of the Sacraments, especially the Holy Eucharist. No matter how she felt during the week, when Sunday came, we were always seated in the second row at Mass. I gleaned my faith from watching my mother pray fervently. My father had a strong faith as well and I recall him being a lector. He was the church organist when he was single. I loved Mass, receiving Communion and the peace we had for one hour. I longed that this normalcy would last.

I witnessed a devout faith and fervent prayer life from my mother who herself suffered relentlessly with undiagnosed health problems. I empathized with her desire to have the quality of health of my aunts and her friends. Yet often she was incapacitated in bed with migraine headaches, body aches, depression, and unrelenting fatigue.

My first job at 14 -15 was an over-the-counter waitress at the local Dairy Queen. I worked from 50 cents an hour up to 95 cents when I was the manager. One of the perks of this job was all the ice cream you could sample. Another was meeting the young, handsome male Air National Guardsmen stationed outside the city limits at Phelps Collins Air Base, now closed due to military cutbacks. My baby blue electric eyes, flirtatious smile, and my inherited good looks helped me secure a few precarious dates. A lesson was quickly learned from these occasions. I learned to say "No" loud and clear to those oh so cute and clever "fly boys." I was growing up but knew better than to compromise my principles.

Next, I became a cashier. I worked mornings at a local department store, similar to a K-Mart, in the mornings. Then I'd ride my bike across town to The Drugstore where I again would check people out at the cash register. I was often thought of as a twin because so many people saw me at both stores! My goal was to save money for cute school clothes, every teenage girl's dream.

In high school, I was passionate about getting good grades, always taking college-prep courses. I planned on attending college after high school. I graduated 50th in my class of 500 students. I didn't think this was too bad as all of the classes I took were a real challenge.

I learned to down-hill ski in junior high. I was self-taught and became very good at the sport. My mom and dad did come to the local ski resort, Mt. Maria, to see me ski once. I remember that it was quite an effort for her. After she died, my father would give me the car to go skiing all the way across the state to Boyne Highlands, or to Gaylord, which was halfway across the state. Some days, I would take my younger brother and sister, and other times, friends from school. I remember one snow day dad let me go to Gaylord and I got stuck in a farmer's long driveway when I stopped to get directions. Even though his wife said he was sick, he came and pushed us out of the deep snow. He wouldn't take the dollar I offered him!

Even through our married years, skiing was the sport we enjoyed as a family. We had several ski trips to Colorado. One achievement just after we were married was becoming a ski instructor at a nearby ski resort. This was a true accomplishment. The lessons to qualify were the only lessons I ever had. My husband, Gary, was proud of me and I was also proud of myself.

I was elated when I would get dates for the homecomings and proms! My moods varied from lows to highs, even in my teens. Never did I get out of control that required medical attention, however.

During my sophomore year of high school, I went for a long weekend to visit my older sister in Ann Arbor. When I returned from this trip, one of my best friends totally ignored me. There was no explanation whatsoever. She just wouldn't talk to me, or even look at me, for that matter. I was devastated and heartbroken.

During the summer between junior and senior years in H.S., a good friend I knew since Jr. High invited me to go with her to Grand Rapids, MI. I met her when the parochial schools did shared time with the public schools. Well, Kelly wanted me to go with her to a river raft event where her boyfriend lived. She had her own Volkswagen van and all! Off we went with my dad's consent. We arrived to the park full of teenagers! Tents were set up for blocks. It was what I had imagined Woodstock was like. There was a lot of drinking, pot smoking, and probably other drugs as they were quite prevalent in those years. The rafting event started on Saturday. Teams had to make a raft out of anything they thought would float the farthest down the river. The one who made it the farthest was declared the winner. Our cardboard contraption didn't go very far, but it was fun participating. The next day I insisted on going to church. Much to their chagrin they drove me to a Catholic Church so I could "Keep Holy the Lord's Day." I attended Mass as they waited the hour outside the church.

In the spring of my junior year, I noticed a very cute boy in the hallway between classes. I had never seen him before but was determined to meet him. I started to say "hi" when we passed. Shortly, we talked and he asked me out on a date. My modus operandi was to secure a date for the prom. When he did ask me, I remember running to the lunchroom commons excitedly to share this news with my girlfriends. Needless to say, after the prom, I didn't even like him. Come to find out, he broke up with his girlfriend because of my flirting with him. I felt guilty and ashamed of my behavior.

13

The summer before I went away to college I met three boys from Flint, the city where I would be moving. We exchanged phone numbers. The next day one of them called me and invited me to go camping with them and two other girls at Interlochen State Park near Traverse City. This was a very enticing invitation. I had never camped before as a family or with other friends. Well, I told my dad I was going. He adamantly objected. This was after my mother had passed. I insisted I was going saying I would have to make decisions for myself in one month's time when I was on my own at school. Well, the day came, and I went, much to his dismay and anger. We had fun swimming all day. We had a bonfire at night and drank until I was sick. Luckily, the guy I was paired up with didn't make advances at me once I told him, "Don't touch me" before I fell fast asleep.

The next morning, I had them take me into Traverse City so I could attend Mass. Lucky for me, the pastor there had been our parish church pastor and knew me. I said he could vouch for me if my dad ever asked him if I were at church that Sunday.

My guidance counselor discouraged me from becoming a teacher due to the job market, so I decided to follow in my sister's footsteps and become a nurse. I once volunteered as a candy striper but thought passing out water was not much service. I was never really sure I wanted to work as a nurse. The only experience I had was caring for my mother before she died.

I did say there was stress on the home-front. My parents were estranged during my high school years although still living under the same roof. They had always had their "ups and downs" but this was more serious. Mom wanted my father to be more communicative and compassionate. The Catholic Family Movement that they belonged to at one time encouraged this type of relationship. When she was well mentally, she strived to attain and maintain a God-centered, married lifestyle. Plus, as most women do, she wanted to confide her feelings, bare her soul to her husband. This did not happen.

At the same time, my father wanted his wife of nearly 23 years to have some semblance of health. He was worn out and turning to the beer bottle to cope. Raising six children, working full-time as a Prudential Insurance agent, and keeping up with the image of "Father of the Year," an award he received in 1964, was not an easy task. He had ambivalent feelings towards a wife who was always sick, even though the doctors said there was nothing wrong. He felt a sense of hostility towards her, which provoked guilt within him. My perceptiveness at 16 picked up on this situation.

Dad was a stocky man at 52 years and a workaholic. I guess he needed to be in order to provide for six children. He was not a man with whom you could share feelings. I knew that from our volatile relationship when I was a young child. My mom and dad fought much of the time, even in front of us children. Neither could communicate their differences calmly and eventually, if not rapidly, things escalated to shouting and shoving matches. Sooner or later, a parish priest would be called to the house for counseling per Mom's request. It never had any lasting results because the underlying problem of mom's health never improved. They both did the best they could as parents under the duress circumstances. But I must say, I was much closer to my mother and had more empathy for her plight than for my father. He just didn't seem to grasp the fact that she was suffering, not only physically, but emotionally as well. I saw this.

The Gift

ONE OF THE MOST PLEASANT EXPERIENCES IN MY LIFE WAS A day spent with my mom when I was a 16-year-old teen. I had just passed through the "I'm so embarrassed of you, Mom phase." Just to let you know how bad it was, I would duck down in the car as we drove through the downtown so none of my peers would see me with her. I then moved into, "I'm so proud to call you Mom" phase. I thank God for my early maturity.

As I was finishing my sophomore year at Alpena High School, my mother was undergoing every imaginable test to diagnose her abdominal pain. All the tests were negative, but her pain persisted. Her doctor planned on admitting her to the hospital for observation.

As one might expect, being the fourth of six children in a dysfunctional home, my individual attention ranged from slim to none. The morning I heard these words from my dear hurting mother, I was put into a state of frozen shock. She calmly, matter-of-factly stated, "Margie, you're going to need clothes for school this fall. Tomorrow you and I will drive to Saginaw (two hours away!) to Fashion Square Mall and go shopping!" She wanted to take me, Margaret Ann, shopping, while still experiencing bouts of abdominal pain? I wasn't sure if I should be so selfish and accept this invitation or reject the offer and swallow the disappointment. Quickly, though, my inner voice and her adamant decision put the plans into action. Still in a state of disbelief, I gathered my money from the savings account at the local bank. Thanking God that I had been prudent with my frivolous spending, I counted a sum of $125 dollars! What could you get for that today?! At that time, though, I knew I could find a few essentials to add to my wardrobe with this cash.

Most overcome by being chosen to spend the whole day with my mother, I was on my best behavior. I did not want to do anything to cause a change of heart on mom's decision. Never before had I received this experience, just the two of us, her and me. Another sibling or two were always in tow for whatever excursion. I could barely fathom the idea of the special attention I yearned for over the years was going to manifest. Within 24 hours it was lavished upon me. Little did ANYONE know how I longed for this individual attention and unconditional love. The memory of this day so long ago still lingers fresh in my mind. The significance of the event had yet to be realized.

A naturally attractive, smartly dressed 50-year old-woman, petite and a trim 125 pounds with her 16-year-old look-alike daughter entered the mall at opening hours. My shoulder length, dark brown hair bounced along with my step and perpetual smile. We combed the stores from one end of the mall to the other. I perused the racks of clothes at almost every store. I tried things on once and sometimes twice before making any hasty and critical decisions. For the first time in my life, I valued my mother's opinion! "Wrong color," "too tight," "too long," "too short," "too expensive," "very cute," were all comments that a year prior would have sent me into a moody fit. A wink, a nod, a frown, a smile were all welcomed affirmations. Something had come over me, and the same something had come over her! She was patient with my indecisiveness. She was tolerant while her pain resumed. She was affirming as I chose one article of clothing and omitted another selection. In retrospect, it had to have been the Holy Spirit that had descended upon us, and everyone we encountered that day.

My savings bought me a great number of stylish items to add to my fall wardrobe. I found a homecoming dress, a violet denim ankle-length weather coat, a chocolate brown jeans jacket, a brown leather saddle-bag purse, a pair of wool dress slacks and matching sweater, and, of course, a pair of jeans! Mom may have contributed a little cash; I really don't recall. We were both exhausted when we headed north for Alpena!

It was a remarkable Mother-Daughter Day of Bonding. Love and affirmations were exchanged: hers to me, and mine to her. A whole day of unconditional, uninterrupted love was shared between us. I could hardly soak it all in as the beauty of it was all-encompassing. I have thanked God for this gift many times since that summer of 1971! The greatest gift, aside from life itself, had been bestowed upon me from her that day. I was uncertain of her love for me before that experience. In that one day she expressed her true feelings of love to me, her second daughter. Thank you, Mom, for a memorable and lasting gift. This day our relationship was healed.

Mom's Last Illness

WITHIN ONE WEEK OF OUR SUCCESSFUL DAY AT FASHION Square Mall, my mother, Imelda A. (Brousseau) Fanslow, was admitted to Alpena General Hospital for observation and tests. The abdominal pain ensued and she found little relief from whatever they were injecting into her every four hours. A month of tests all indicated no cause for her body wracked with pain, a distended abdomen, and a misery-ridden face. A transfer to the mental health ward was indicated as her diagnosis was "conclusively psychosomatic."

Since my parents were virtually estranged although living under the same roof, she did not want Dad to visit her in the hospital. As I was the oldest child at home, at age 16, I became the designated visitor. So, every day, after school, I would ride my royal blue Schwinn bike a mile to visit Mom. Needless to say, I found a "drugged mother" upon my arrival. The ritual was arriving at the psych ward, getting buzzed in, and waiting for her to come to the visitors' lounge. I observed my loving, expressive, sometimes passionate to volatile mother walk somberly, glassy eyed towards me, down the cold corridor. She was lost to me inside a mind altered by "medicine." It was dehumanizing for her and draining on her designated caregiver, namely, me. Even at a young age, I could see no progress in this month-long admission. I wondered if she would ever come out of the drunken stupor and return to a real person with her old personality. Her spirit was waning. I worried and prayed.

My three older siblings had already left the nest by this time. They lived from two to five hours away. Finally, Mom agreed to let Dad visit. It was strained. They were not "in relationship." My sister and brothers visited once or twice. One day, she was given a day pass. The plan was for me to drive her one and a half hours north to Mackinac City for the day. Paula, 8, and Gerry, 12, accompanied me. I remember going into a restaurant with the three of them and ordering pancakes. Mom was like a zombie, falling asleep in her chair. Finally, she excused herself to go to the car and sleep. I made sure she was in the vehicle before I rejoined my little brother and sister. Needless to say, we returned to the hospital after one stressful day. Just what a 16-year-old child should have the responsibility to do!

For one week after her discharge with a decrease in psychotropic drugs, some of her true self emerged. She was still sullen and depressed and exhibited a flat affect. I was determined to make her feel better. I celebrated her fiftieth birthday by presenting her with an engraved sterling silver charm with 10-16-21 inscribed, to add to her much treasured charm bracelet. She lay in the fetal position on the sofa to receive her gift. I remember telling her, "I was going to have inscribed, 'Half a Century.'" She quipped with half a smile, "That would make me sound so old!" At that time, I thought she must feel more like a hundred years than her true fifty. She was still experiencing pain and I felt uncertain of a full recovery. This was a real-life nightmare. There was nothing I could do but pray.

One week post discharge from the psyche ward, the crisis began. It was Sunday morning, and I went to Mass with my brother and sister. Dad stayed home with mom. Upon returning, Mrs. Hayes, our babysitter and my mom's good and loyal friend, greeted me at the door. She was like a nanny to us children throughout the years. I knew something terrible had happened while we were at church. As Mrs. Hayes explained, my mother hemorrhaged both from the mouth and the rectum. Dad called the ambulance and went with her to the hospital. Immediately, I drove to the ER to see her. I met dad as she had just been taken to emergency surgery. The report was a perforated ulcer. Her prognosis was poor. She had lost a lot of blood and had many blood transfusions. She was in ICU when I saw her next.

The rest of the family was summoned. A week of continuous waiting, praying, hoping, and visits at her bedside was what we experienced as she lay in a semi-comatose state. This went on from Sunday until Friday night. The nurses sent my sister, Mary Ellen, her fiancé, Tom, and myself home for a break. My dad, my Uncle Emiel, and my mother's friend, Virginia, were at her bedside. No sooner did we get home the phone rang. I knew it was the hospital. I was right. We raced back but she had already passed. The Holy Spirit prepared me for this loss throughout her earlier stages of the illness. Again I had a little voice in my head tell me she would never return home to us again. In some ways, it was a relief for there would no longer be the dysfunction that went with her illness. I knew she would no longer suffer from the horrendous and crippling mood swings. Yet I grieved and longed for her for years. A week after her 50th birthday, October 22, 1971, God's will to end her suffering prevailed.

After we were home, my dad relayed the story of her final moments before her last breath. She rose up in bed from a week of being in a semi-comatose state. She had one last bequest. She explained that there was $50 dollars in her coat pocket in the front closet. This money was to be sent to the Capuchin Monastery on Mt. Elliott in Detroit, Michigan that night. She was emphatic! The intention was for Masses to be said for vocations to the priesthood. This is where Blessed Fr. Solanus Casey had been stationed for the latter part of his life. He is nearing canonization to sainthood in the Catholic Church today. This was a miraculous event.

The events stated above had much significance. As the story was always told, mom had a healing through the intercession of Fr. Solanus while she was pregnant with me. All of her childhood and adult life she suffered with inner ear problems. A doctor told her she would need surgery after she delivered her baby. A blessing with the relic of the cross of Christ and prayers said over her in person from Fr. Solanus healed her ear disease. After she delivered me, the same doctor examined her ear again. He could not believe what he saw. Her ear was completely healed. This was a miracle.

The day after her death on Saturday morning, I attended Mass with my father. I had a divine moment. As I knelt in prayer with closed eyes, it was as if a baton, like one from a relay race, was suddenly whirled through the air into my hands. I opened my eyes to see what had happened and realized it was a mystical moment of sorts. I truly believe the Holy Spirit was passing on to me my mother's faith, perseverance, and love to share with others. It was definitely a surreal and providential experience.

The funeral followed one week later. I never had a chance to say goodbye. I knew that she was finally at peace in the presence of our Heavenly Father. The Mass was beautiful, and St. Mary Church was filled to capacity.

I have treasured in my heart our "special shopping day" since the time it occurred. It was God's gift from her to me. We had reconciled our relationship during that brief encounter. With one quick blink of an eye, she was lost to me forever. Presumptuously I believe He knew I needed this blessing from her to go forward without regret after her death. I was given time to make amends with her and gain forgiveness from her personally, and from God, for all of the sins against her that I had incurred during my rebellious teenage years. Thanks to God, I was guilt-free and at peace for the rest of my life.

God gave me empathy at an early age. He gave me a spiritual, faith-filled mother who discerned His will. These traits were passed to me through example, grace, and prayer. She told me before she was admitted to the hospital that she would never return to live in this house again. I interpreted it to be because of my parent's relationship. Yet God was calling her home and preparing my sensitive heart with incomprehensible words. He rescued her from mental, physical, and emotional pain. Her love still flows from above with the communion of saints. God left me with an undying love for Him and belief in His healing powers.

When my mother died, my youngest sister was only eight and I took her under my wing. I gave her all the "motherly" love and attention that I craved and intuitively knew a child needed. I was the one who told her that Mom went to heaven. During the months that followed, I would often console her as she cried at bedtime. I resented my dad and thought his behavior contributed to Mom's illness and death.

I taught Paula to downhill ski, enrolled her in swim classes, gymnastic lessons, and piano lessons. I supported and encouraged her in these endeavors. These were only some of the things I had wished for as a child. Today, I know my parents did the best they knew how in raising me, but it took years of counseling and forgiveness to accept this fact.

College Years

I CHOSE A NURSING SCHOOL IN FLINT, MICHIGAN, ABOUT THREE hours south of my hometown after high school. One of the main reasons I chose Hurley Medical Center School of Nursing was G.M.I. (now Kettering University) which was also located in Flint. It was an all-male school whose young men socialized with the Hurley nurses! This is what clinched my decision. At least I'd have a social life outside the books.

The G.M.I. fraternities had parties on the weekends that the nursing students attended. It was a drinking bash and a dance to live music. This was a relief from the intense school schedule we endured. I always made it to church on Sunday even though we partied hard on Saturday night.

During the three years of a tough curriculum and clinical experiences, I began cycling from low tones to then high energy levels. I remember a conversation with my classmates about our personalities. I described myself as being really high or really low. I managed to maintain my sanity throughout the extreme stress of this program. The day I graduated as a Registered Nurse was one of the happiest days of my life. I had achieved a milestone of a goal, my mood was exceptionally positive, and this stressor was removed from my life! For many years in my adult life, I had nightmares that I was still in school! I would dream that this could not be true. When I awoke and realized it was not real, I was extremely relieved.

In the fall of 1974, I ended a year-long relationship with a GMI guy. I finally realized he was just using me and I knew he was not someone whom

I wanted to spend the rest of my life with. I walked to his fraternity and read him the riot act right in the living room along with sobbing tears. After that episode, I asked if he could at least drive me back to my dormitory. He did oblige.

That relationship was pulling me down the wrong path in life. He never wanted to do anything except drink and smoke pot. Also he was making sexual advances which I complied with to a limit. I never had sex with him but did things I now am ashamed to admit. Luckily, he was only at school for six weeks at a time. The next six weeks he went to his home in Ohio for his co-op work assignment, so it wasn't even a whole year that we dated.

While at Hurley I did date many fraternity brothers from General Motors Institute. But let me tell you another providential story. One evening during the week, although I never went out as a rule Sunday nights through Thursday, I was convinced by some girls to go to a fraternity for a short visit and a practical joke. Believe me, I did not have much of a sense of humor back then, but eventually went along. While in the foyer of the fraternity waiting for my friends, a young bearded guy walked passed me and glanced my way. We never spoke. He vanished into another room as quickly as he had entered. A whispered voice in my head said, "You are going to marry that man." My thought response, although startled, was, "Yeah, right."

Needless to say, a few weeks later a group of Hurley girls went skiing to Mt. Holly with a group of G.M.I. guys. I was introduced to Gary there. I noticed he had his own skis but paid no attention other than that factor. Skiing was my sport and I just figured if he didn't have rentals, he at least knew how to ski. A few weeks later, he asked me out on a date to a concert. I had a fine time. Upon returning home, he asked me to go ice-skating the following weekend. This was another sport I loved as well since I spent my childhood on skates, growing up in Northern Michigan. The reaction to this invitation was that there was hope for a relationship with this guy.

We bonded readily. I soon took him home to meet my dad and younger brother, Gerry, 16, and baby sister, Paula who was now twelve. That weekend although I was only twenty, I recall telling my dad that I would one day marry Gary. It wasn't until months later while looking at his picture did I remember the words of the Holy Spirit and the face of the young man I saw in the fraternity foyer. It was Gary who had passed in front of me when I heard the whisper in my ear, "You're going to marry that man." Again, I was amazed by this revelation.

Gary and I got engaged at Christmas of 1975. When I returned to school after break, I remember a sad occasion. I went to a friend's room to announce our wedding date. She, too, had gotten engaged. Coincidentally we had both chosen the same date for our weddings. I was disappointed as we shared many of the same friends. As I was leaving her room, another girl who was there said, "I wouldn't go to that crazy girl's wedding, don't worry." It hurt when many of my friends went to her wedding instead of mine. Since I had other friends outside of "The little sisters of the fraternity of ATO," many of my other girlfriends from Hurley Medical Center of Nursing did attend our wedding. Although it was bittersweet, it did not dampen my joyous day. Years later, I heard that the other couple divorced. With all we had endured, we were still happily married.

So, we dated from January of 1975, and got engaged at Christmas of 1975. We knew quite soon into our relationship that we were meant for each other and it was God's destiny. He graduated the year before me so that meant only seeing him on weekends. We were intensely in love. Although being very difficult we saved ourselves until our wedding night. We wrote love letters every day when he returned to his hometown. I so looked forward for the mail each day. He visited every weekend. Not long ago, we found the box of his letters to me in our storage room. It was a sentimental moment.

Wedding

ONE OF THE HAPPIEST DAYS OF MY LIFE WAS OUR WEDDING day, October 9th, 1976. It was a day I didn't expect to happen at such a young age as I was just 21. However, I believed God had a design for my life which I had to obey. It really was as if Gary and I were born for each other. We each helped each other grow in different ways as we journeyed along our paths in life.

Before I walked up the aisle escorted by my father, he looked at me and said "Are you sure?" I replied "I am." I felt peaceful, calm, and confident in my decision to receive the sacrament of Holy Matrimony. When I look back, we were two innocent kids in love with a strong determination to keep our love alive and be true to our vows we pledged to each other. My faith was strong and I knew it. Although Gary was a non-Catholic, he had more faith than either of us really knew or understood.

Our ceremony was beautiful and very personal. I could feel the presence of the Holy Spirit. We chose our music and readings to be spiritual and meaningful. I remember two of the songs we selected. First, the *Prayer of St. Francis* and *Let There be Peace on Earth and Let it Begin With Me*. The second song was so our marriage would bring a peaceful life unlike the one I witnessed growing up as a child. I remember taking a bouquet of flowers to the altar of the Blessed Mother. My dad played a Polish song on the organ and three members of the choir sang along. They were so out of tune it took everything we had to not giggle.

We recited the traditional vows and were joyfully united as man and wife. God's love radiated throughout my whole body. My confirmation sponsor (my second cousin) said to me after the ceremony, "Margie, I felt a special feeling during the service." I was speechless.

Our reception was a fun-filled party with me as the hostess. It was held at a VFW hall with no attached frills. I came alive from a shy little girl to a vibrant bride. I visited with our friends and family and thoroughly enjoyed myself. I originally wanted a trio of musicians for dancing, but Dad found a Polish band to entertain the crowd. I danced one polka after another with all of our guests. That was one of the prerequisites before we got married, for Gary to learn to dance a Polka! We had a grand time and I recall it and all of the events that took place as if it were yesterday.

I realized that night that there were many differences between our two families. Mine were more social, his more reserved. For a fleeting moment, "I thought, what am I getting myself into?" To this day, we are closer to my family and celebrate more holidays and events with them. I still love his family, though. I could never call his mother, "Mom', or anything for that goes, for it was only five short years since my mom had died and I still grieved her loss. Once our son was born, I referred to her as Grandma.

I felt Gary's love for me and believed he was sincere in his promises to me as a husband. As the years progressed, nothing could be more evident. Our love was unconditional from the very beginning.

Our wedding night was spent at the nicest motel in Alpena. The "best" room was a deer hunter's special including mounted deer heads on the walls! We laughed about it but did not let the room's motif ruin our first intimate experience. Our lovemaking was in its infant stages but grew in leaps and bounds during our honeymoon and the years to follow.

Since I had just been at my job for two months I could only have a long weekend off for our honeymoon. We chose Gatlinburg, Tennessee and the Smoky Mountains for our destination. Gary drove the whole way and I slept. All of our clothes were hanging on a bar in the back seat. Well, since there was champagne left over from our wedding night, I corked it up and put it on the floor in the back seat. When we arrived at the hotel, the wine bottle exploded and sprayed over the back seat. Our clothes were spared, but I found this to be hilarious and could not contain my laughter! Needless to say, Gary did not see the humor in the incident since he was exhausted from driving the whole trip. I witnessed some of his anger for the first time.

We had a special few days of hiking the trails and enjoying the views from the mountain summits. Needless to say, many of our vacations over the years have included hiking, even now into our senior years.

My first nursing job was in a little community in Grosse Pointe Farms, Michigan. Cottage Hospital was the first place of employment as an R.N. after nursing school in 1976. I liked the fact that it was small compared to the 11-floor hospital where I had studied. I worked the midnight shift. I could not tolerate the hours. I would nearly fall asleep on the drive home, sleep all day, and want to go back to bed when it got dark. I called in sick several times in the six months that I worked there. I told my supervisors that I could not stay awake to work this shift. There were no day shifts available. So, after six or seven months, I resigned. This was a depressed state that I did not recognize. My body could not adjust to the sleep change. I resigned from this job after only six months as I was falling into a depression and sleeping round the clock. Although I was in the medical field and had studied psychiatric nursing, never did I relate my symptoms to being a mental illness. I figured I had a good husband, a career, money, and faith, and no reason to be depressed. After we took a vacation to sunny, warm Florida, my mood lifted.

Shortly after we returned from vacation, I went to St. John Hospital and insisted on a day position when I interviewed. They were insistent that there were no day shifts available. I was emphatic that I only could work days because my husband worked days. Lo and behold, a supervisor came in and gave me a day position on a medical/surgical floor. I fit in with the staff and felt really good about my career. I worked in that capacity until I had my first manic episode. For the last three years of my employment there, I was assigned to a high-risk, post-partum floor where I remained until I resigned around 1988.

Amy Nicole

AT AGE 24, I YEARNED FOR A BABY. I GOT PREGNANT AS SOON as we tried. The pregnancy was normal. I planned on delivering in a home-like birthing center adjacent to a hospital. The pregnancy went along smoothly with only mild nausea in the first trimester. In my seventh month and 32 weeks gestation, I was at work. As the head cardiac surgeon and I were charting towards the end of my shift, he asked me how I was. I replied, "If I knew what it was like, I'd say I was in labor right now." I had been cramping all afternoon but attributed it to the corned beef sandwich I ate at lunch. By the time I drove home I was having severe contractions. Immediately I called the doctor and he advised me to call an ambulance and go to a hospital. We were several miles from the hospital I was to deliver at and the only route was surface streets with many traffic lights. There were no freeways across town at that time. I chose to wait for Gary as I expected him home quite soon. We left for the hospital the moment he arrived. By this time, I knew something was wrong and the time it took to reach the hospital seemed like forever.

Within minutes of arriving in labor and delivery, without even stopping at E.R. my water broke and I had to push. They sent Gary out to register me. It was a precipitous delivery. Our baby girl was only two and a half pounds and severely cyanotic when she was born. There was no cry. The doctor proceeded to give me a D&C to remove the placenta. A nurse wrapped the baby in a blanket and brought her to my bedside. I did not know if she were living or not. I touched her cold cheek and looked at her beautiful, tiny features and dark hair.

The nurse never offered me the opportunity to hold her and I did not even know enough to ask. She was baptized Amy Nicole Graham by a nurse. Then I was wheeled to a labor room where the tears began to flow. By then my attending doctor had arrived at the scene. He told me she had a birth defect, omphalocele, and I would not want to see it. Evidently the abdominal wall did not develop and her organs were exposed. I asked why I was still in this room and he said she had a strong heart. Then I realized she had not died yet. I still was not offered the opportunity to hold her or bond with her. To this day, I mourn her loss and the lack of closure.

The birth and death of our first born daughter, Amy Nicole, was the most painful loss I had ever experienced, even worse than my mother's death. That was September 5th or 6th of 1979. I can never remember the exact date it was so traumatic. To this day, I can reenact the whole scene as if it were in a sad movie.

She was a baby well longed for and loved even before she was conceived. I was in shock when I was admitted to a room on the post-partum floor. Babies could be heard crying and the other women in the room were brought their babies to hold. I made a few calls to family and friends before Gary left for home. The loss he felt was different than what I experienced. I carried that baby in my womb as part of my life.

That night I sobbed continuously. A woman in the next bed tried to console me. By the time morning arrived, I was more than ready to be discharged. As soon as my doctor came in to make rounds and Gary arrived, I was wheeled out of the maternity ward without a baby. This was gut-wrenching to say the least.

For whatever reason, I chose not to have a funeral. I was so distraught and had no experience in picking cemeteries, caskets, or making such arrangements. I did decide on a funeral home and picked the same cemetery where Gary's dad had been buried. I did not even know there was a Catholic cemetery in the area. A priest came and said a few prayers as Gary and I stood by with the undertaker holding a box with our baby inside. I didn't even have a Mass said for her until a few years afterwards. We never did put a stone on her resting place. The circumstances were surreal.

A few friends came to console us in the next few days. My family all lived out of the area so I only talked to them on the telephone. My dad, Paula, and

Mary Ellen did come to visit and console me. The grief was immense. I just sat in the family room in a daze and shed tears for days. Gary kept busy working on the car and on odd jobs. Men and women grieve differently. He tried to comfort me though in his own way.

I questioned my faith in God. I could not understand how He could give me this cross to bear at such a young age. With hindsight, though, I think it would have been worse to have a child with brain damage who would require care for many years. Even after 40 years, I still have dreams that I am pregnant. I wake up with a sad feeling in my heart. My mothering instincts were never fulfilled.

At my six-week follow up appointment with my O.B. doctor, everything was normal. I was still sad but coping. At that time he suggested we wait for six or more months to try again for another baby. With prayer guiding me, I put this decision in God's hands instead. I was expecting in three months. I yearned for life in me again. Amy's never been replaced in my heart. I love her but know I will be reunited with her in eternal life.

For this second pregnancy, I decided not to work for fear of another devastating outcome. I took a one-year leave of absence. By my sixth month of pregnancy, I was starting to dilate and was put on bed rest. Paula, who is nine years younger than me, came to our rescue. She agreed to come to spend the summer. I was able to stay on the couch while she cooked, cleaned, did laundry, including ironing Gary's work shirts. What a big help she was! She stayed until I delivered and was the first to meet our son, Shaun Robert.

First Manic Episode — 1980

A SPECIAL BIBLE PASSAGE I CLUNG TO DURING THOSE TIMES WAS Matthew 8:23-27 Storm on the Lake. "He got into a boat and his disciples followed him. Suddenly a violent storm came up on the sea, so that the boat was being swamped by waves, but he was asleep. They came and woke him, saying "Lord save us! We are perishing!" He said to them, 'Why are you terrified, O you of little faith?" Then he got up, rebuked the winds and the sea, and there was great calm. The men were amazed and said, "What sort of man is this whom even the winds and the sea obey?" The storm in our marriage has been my bipolar illness, previously known as manic-depressive illness.

In August of 1980, we brought our son home from the hospital, just eleven months after burying our first-born baby girl. My husband and I sat on the floor of the nursery and cried tears of joy and relief. After two years of pregnancy, we finally had a baby.

Within the next few weeks, I felt like I was a wild animal who was just released from a cage. I had more energy than usual and required less sleep than normal. I began buying large quantities of fruits and vegetables, blanching and pureeing for fresh baby food. I also took on household projects that were extreme. My mood was elevated. I was going through my first hypo-manic episode, although I was unaware of what was happening.

When the baby was six weeks old, he was baptized. We had a big party with family and friends. Some people at the party observed my behavior as abnormal. However, they did not share this information with my husband. Had they done so, Gary could have at least been aware of the situation and watched me more closely.

I was eager to take my baby to my place of employment, St. John's Hospital in Detroit to show him to my co-workers. So, one day, I dressed in the only dress that fit and set off on our outing. As I drove down I-94, I was singing, "Be not Afraid, I go before you, come follow me and I will give you rest" very loudly. When we got to visit my nurse friends, I still had the presence of mind to behave normally. No one suspected I was getting sick mentally.

However, once I was on my way home, I decided to go visit an LPN who lived in the city of Detroit. The only thing was I had no idea where she lived. I drove through different neighborhoods and stopped at random houses and asked if Roberta lived there. This was insane. Then I stopped at a cemetery and walked around with my son in my arms looking at various religious headstones. An employee asked me, "Are you ok, miss?" I answered, "I'm ok, you ok?" as that was a popular book and saying at that time. Then I drove around the city and did not know my whereabouts.

I ended up stopping in front of a store-front church with several people of African American decent outside. I took the baby from the car seat, and began talking to these strangers. One older man said, "Let me drive you somewhere." By this time I had slipped mentally to total confusion. So I went with him. When we got to a house he immediately went to a bedroom. I was irrational.

I remember being on a balcony holding my son and feeling like Abraham with Isaac. I would do anything God wanted me to do even if he wanted me to drop the baby over the railing. I heard a whisper in my mind, "Do not hurt the baby." The weekend progressed and my memory of it is sketchy. I remember talking loudly like I was going to save the Black girls and then being hit with a baseball bat on my legs to shut-up. This happened during the night. I lost any memory of where the baby was during the rest of the weekend. Other people came to the house to see this stranger who just happened to show up on a Friday afternoon. They stole my diamond wedding band. I remember trying to call home but could not remember my phone number.

Now, this is what was happening back at my house from Friday night until Sunday night. Gary arrived home from work to find the house unlocked. The dog was missing but soon returned by a neighbor. Gary started to call friends and relatives to try and find me. He became frantic as time went by and I was missing. People began looking for me everywhere. Gary was praying continuously and was asking everyone for prayers that I would be found.

My two older brothers, Bob and Ron from Michigan, came and helped in the search. A friend, Joe from Marriage Encounter, who grew up in Detroit, offered his help. Gary had an inspiration. He knew I had been acting very religious during this phase of my illness. He recalled that I had been watching a TV program broadcast from an evangelical church in Detroit. He found the whereabouts of this place and suggested looking there. My car was a bright orange Mercury Comet with a World Wide Marriage Encounter sticker in the back window. As my friend and brothers drove around the east side of Detroit, they spotted my car. Two men got in. Joe followed the car which led them to the house where I was staying for the whole weekend. Finding a phone booth, my brother called the police.

The next thing I remember is a female police officer coming into the house, taking the baby from a woman who had been holding him. She grabbed me and took me out of the house. In the confusion of the police arriving, I remember the men leaving in a hurry through the back door.

The police gave me and the baby to my brother. One of them drove my car home with Shaun in his car seat. The baby was fine. Whoever else was at the house must have fed and cared for him. He was checked out by the pediatrician the following day and was in good condition.

I recall being famished. Joe stopped at a McDonald's. I proceeded to eat more than one Big Mac. I had not eaten the entire weekend.

As we arrived to my house, Gary was in tears. I was talking out of my mind. I had hallucinated and was confused with regards to time, place, and person. Gary was grateful that I was alive.

After a night in ER at a Jewish hospital, I was adamant about getting out of there. I thought the world was coming to an end and we would not be saved if we were there! This was insanity. My brother Gerry was present to console me.

I was admitted to Glenn Eden, a psychiatric hospital. I was completely out of my mind, not even knowing my name. I remember another patient showed me my wristband and telling me, "You are Margaret Graham."

After three weeks or more and many drugs, I finally came back to somewhat of a realistic state of mind while in the doctor's office during our session. I did not know where I was or what had happened at the time. He enlightened me of my episode. Then he proceeded to tell me that I could not have any more children because of the side effects of Lithium, the drug I was being prescribed. Lithium was known to cause life-threatening heart defects. I was devastated. We had wanted a big family and I was only 25 years old.

I was taken to a gynecologist doctor to have an injection to stop the milk production because I had been nursing. Another trip to this office was when I realized I had a vaginal infection. I was still out of my mind. I thought the nurse assisting the doctor during the examination was my mother. I recall embracing her and saying, "I knew you would never leave me, Mom." She just held me for a brief moment until I came back to some semblance of reality. When I started my period during this hospitalization, everyone was relieved. Just what I would have needed was to become pregnant from this horrific experience.

Gradually, I recovered. After every hospitalization, a period of depression followed. Antidepressants were prescribed at these times. It was a trial-and-error process to see which drug worked on this aspect of the disease. It took time to fully recuperate after each hospital stay. Through prayer and meditation and counseling, I recovered. Gary accepted me intimately after this horrendous event. I was healthy and able to return to work when my year leave of absence was finished.

Signs and Symptoms of Bipolar Illness

THE SIGNS AND SYMPTOMS OF BIPOLAR DISEASE CAN VARY. Some other symptoms people often exhibit are racing thoughts, flight of ideas, and paranoia. Daily, I monitor myself to time, place, and person. I evaluate my mood as to being balanced, depressed, or hypo-manic, which is feeling VERY good and creative. I always get a little nervous when I feel too good. Isn't that a sad thought, to feel too good? Hypomania leads to mania and to psychosis in my disease. After years of dealing with hospitalizations we became aware of my trigger signs. One was becoming sneaky. I would do things secretly that I did not want Gary to know about, buy something, or go someplace unusual by myself.

I would get angry with him over little things. He was the brunt of my wrath. I knew Gary's vulnerabilities and insecurities, and I would go out of my way to bring them up. When I did this, he would become attuned to my moods.

Once I adopted a 110 pound dog from a Humane Society two hours north of us and went there and back by myself to pick him up. This was done without even talking about it with Gary. I just wanted another dog and found a rescue through several telephone calls.

I would buy things in large quantities. When I moved into my own massage office, I bought a beautiful desk, credenza, bookshelf, and leather loveseat! As a massage therapist my income was very low, barely enough to pay the bills and buy the supplies.

I never got paranoid, but I know some people do. I used to get forgetful about taking my medications if I were getting sick. However, after the years passed, we finally figured out that Lithium did not control my manias. My doctor didn't adjust my drugs when I was becoming hypomanic. She would allow me to get full blown manic, completely out of my mind. Then she would have me hospitalized. She did not have hospital privileges so would pawn me off on another doctor. They would put me on antipsychotic drugs, and within two weeks, I would return to a sane state of mind. Different drugs were also added to the regime to get me under control and ready for release. I was never completely well, though, when I was discharged. When I returned to my out-patient doctor, I would ask to be put back on Lithium because I felt too drugged. Instead of keeping me on some of the anti-psychotic drugs, she would comply with my wishes and put me back on the Lithium. Within about two to three years, I would cycle up again into another manic phase and the whole scenario would begin again.

After each mania, a depression would follow. I was then put on anti-depressants to counter act this phase of the disease. To be a faith-filled woman with bipolar illness was to my advantage. During these periods, I would spend much time in prayer. I would watch Eternal Word Television Network. I would pray the rosary with Mother Angelica. I would watch Mass on TV, too. This is when I first learned the Divine Mercy Chaplet. When I attended Sunday services, the songs would make me cry as it was so hard to recover from depression. Luckily, I was never hospitalized for this part of the disease.

More Hospitalizations

THE SECOND HOSPITALIZATION TOOK PLACE WHEN MY SON was three. I dropped him off at preschool. I could feel things were getting out of control without much warning. I did go to a friend's house to seek help. She had her husband pick Shaun up from school and we waited for Gary to return from work. Again he called the doctor. She found a bed for me in one of the local psych wards. My very first psychiatric physician had told me there were drugs I could take to alleviate a hospitalization, but I could not articulate that to my current doctor and she was unaware of this treatment.

In the hospital I would do arts and crafts, attend group therapy, sit through free time, do laundry, and in one place, I even had music therapy which I loved. They always had a smoking room at each hospital, too. Although I wasn't a smoker, I would get cigarettes from other patients and get high from smoking. This was about the only time I felt half-way normal. I socialized with other patients at these times.

I was hypo-manic when my son was going into first grade. I remember one funny story from that time. I decided to take him on a shopping trip to the old Hudson's store. We drove to the mall and found the boy's department. Since it was the end of the season everything was on clearance. It was like Christmas in July! He got two different jeans jackets, several shorts and tops sets, and all and all, two big shopping bags of clothes. And a precious teddy bear was bought as well. We left to discover I had locked my keys in the car! This was way before cell phones. I thought, "If Julie Andrews walked out of

Germany over the mountains, we could surely walk home." It was quite far though. It proceeded to rain and our bags were beginning to rip open. I needed help. We were on a commercial road with very few houses. When we came upon one lone farm house, I knocked at the door. An older couple skeptically let me in to use the telephone. With the help of a phone book I found my next door neighbor's number and phoned her. I remember her daughter answering the phone. She said her mother was in the shower. I insisted that it was an emergency and she let me speak to her. With help from the older couple we gave her directions and she came and rescued us. I can laugh at this now, but then it was not so funny.

I worked at Nutri-System weight loss center for four years. I stayed well during that time period. That was shortly after I had resigned from St. John's Hospital. All during these years, I was still seeing my same doctor for medications and therapy. I wanted to go back to work after the weight loss center closed. I did physicals for an insurance company for a brief period of time.

One time when I was admitted to St. Joseph's in Mt. Clemens I had a horrific experience. I was out of my mind while I was being oriented to the ward by a staff member. After putting my belongings into my room I came out and went into the room which I thought was the non-smoking room. Patients were smoking. I was disturbed because I had come to hate smoke. I knocked on the glass window of the office adjacent to this room and said loudly, "They are smoking in here!" Within two seconds, two male attendants came in, grabbed me, and dragged me to solitary confinement. I was left in there a long time. No one checked on me. I had to urinate on the floor. I also scratched onto my arm the letters "AMA." I wanted to leave there against medical advice, but I was stuck there for at least a week. I got discharged early because I had a wedding to go to. I demanded my physician release me. He obliged my demands.

I remember another time I was put in solitary confinement at Cottage Hospital in Grosse Pointe. The staff had to keep all of your cosmetics and anything sharp like a fingernail file. These were referred to as "sharpies." After using them at night, you had to return them to the staff. They searched your cosmetic bag to be sure everything was accounted for. Well, they couldn't find my nail file one night. I was taken to solitary, stripped searched, and locked in for the night on a bare mattress and no blanket. Sometime during the night they came in and said they had found the file. This was a traumatic experience.

I was demoralized, angry, and humiliated. I was allowed to go back to my room without so much as an apology!

Several years after working at Cottage Hospital, I was admitted there a second time for one of my many hospitalizations. I often walked the halls at night because I couldn't sleep. The night nurse told me that my old supervisor was making her rounds and recognized my name on the patient's list. She wanted to see me. So I saw her as I passed by the desk while I walked the halls because I could not sleep. I just remember saying to her, "I told you something was wrong with me." She just looked at me without a reply.

Massage Therapy from 1988 - 1999

IN 1988 WITH THE HELP OF A MICHIGAN WORKS COUNSELOR, I searched for a new career. I do not know how or where I got the idea to become a massage therapist, but that is what I told the counselor. She immediately thought of prostitution. I explained what a massage therapist entailed. We found a school for massage therapy in the area. I applied and was accepted.

Wouldn't you know I got sick that summer before school started in September? Against my family's judgment, I insisted on going anyway. I got permission to start late from the director who also suffered from some sort of mental illness. She was very empathetic. It was the best therapy for me at the time. Not only was I learning to give massages, but I was receiving them on a regular basis. The touch therapy I received from the other students made it a very healing year.

After that year of schooling, I was determined to find a job. Through some contacts I found a chiropractor's office who wanted a therapist. I started right away. When I went to interview for my first massage therapist position, I almost died. The chiropractor was drop dead gorgeous! I was immediately infatuated with him. I told Gary about the situation so I could keep a handle on my emotions. Luckily, I never strayed from our vows.

Gradually, I built up my practice at the clinic. Giving talks at churches, through referrals from the two chiropractors, and by word of mouth, I was giving seven to eight massages a day!

The first five years were spent at the chiropractor's office. It was not the best of work environments. The women employees were mean to me. I could only figure they were jealous of my successful business. The doctors treated me as another professional as I was also an R.N. My patients loved me and I got instant gratification from relieving them of their pain. The next five years I worked in an office by myself. This was much less stressful than putting up with the "cattiness" of the women from the clinic.

When I moved out on my own, I found out that the chiropractic clinic had stolen all of my patients' names and information. Beforehand, though, I had new business cards made and distributed them to all of my patients. I never lost a patient to the clinic's new therapist!

After a couple years of practicing on my own, I again shifted to a manic state of mind. At that time, I had an associate who covered for me while I was in the hospital. I had one patient wanting to schedule an appointment only with me as she had a pre-paid package of six massages. My associate could not appease this woman. Her husband was a lawyer and she threatened to sue me. So I wrote her a letter and explained the situation. Needless to say, she was compassionate while she waited for me to return to the office.

At that time, I decided to inform all of my patients of my illness. Most of them stayed with me and were very empathetic. I was good at deep tissue massages to relieve chronic pain. Since they got good results, they were kind and waited while I recovered. I would return to work ASAP as it seemed to shorten my recovery. I definitely had to push myself, though.

One time when I was getting sick, I went to the clinic after I no longer worked there. I had told the doctor who owned the clinic years before that I was bipolar. I always wanted someone to know in case of an emergency. He was nice enough to call my psychiatrist and find out what medications I should take. Naturally, she told him the same regimen that I was taking daily, which had proven to be ineffective to control my manias. However, they were nice enough to drive me home and stay with me until Gary came home from work. Back to the hospital I went.

One time when I worked in my own office, I left without cancelling my appointments. I remember driving on the expressway, going through little towns and not really knowing where I was. I was in a confused state of mind. I came to a sign for I-94 West and drove back to the office. I was lucky not to get lost again.

August of 1999, I decided to close my business, Massage Therapy Inc. I had just experienced another hospitalization. I was devastated. A big part of my life went missing. Stress was a precursor to my manias and my job was physically and mentally exhausting. I considered my profession my ministry. I had told God I would work as long as I could perform physically, spiritually, and emotionally. It was a sad time as I loved my job, patients, and independence. Satisfaction came with the immediate gratification I experienced from relieving others of chronic pain. I felt pride in my work. I was loved by my patients. It was a sad time to have to retire at such a young age without warning. I lost my connections with all those people that I served for years.

The years I worked as a massage therapist were quite rewarding for me. In addition to being a good massage therapist, I was a good listener. During my years as a massage therapist, many people who became steady patients confided in me. They too had suffered losses, depression, and other similar circumstances like my own. When it was appropriate, I would share with them parts of my life that were similar. I was able to empathize with their ordeals. I developed many close relationships.

Last Manic Episode

In February of 2000, I decided one day to take a "business trip." I didn't need to travel because I had already closed my massage therapy business. I figured if my husband could fly to another city for a day, so could I. Using my frequent flyer miles, I managed to reserve a two-way ticket to Atlanta GA for that very day. I remember it was Ash Wednesday, the first day of the Lenten Season in the Catholic Church. Our plan was to go to 7PM Mass and receive our ashes as a couple.

I made my reservations for mid-morning and a return trip for midafternoon. I found the day parking lot at Detroit's Metro airport and this was my go-ahead. I "decided if I could find the day parking lot God would take care of me and I was well enough to make it there safely and return safely."

I remember sitting by the window of the plane in awe of the beauty of the earth from the sky. Every sensation in a hypo-manic state is of heightened awareness. Everything and everyone was beautiful. When I arrived at Atlanta's airport I went to a bar/restaurant and had breakfast. I remember sitting alone at the bar eating eggs and toast. My eyes glanced at the liquor bottles lining the wall ahead of me. I was tempted to have a drink. The thought in my head prompted me not to. That was a good decision.

Afterwards, I headed for the pay telephones. I tried to find an old girlfriend's phone number but failed. I was able to find her ex-husband's law firm's phone number, dialed it, and left a message. I still had the presence of mind to stay at the airport near my gate so I wouldn't miss my return flight home or get lost in a strange city. I passed the time by visiting with strangers which was totally out of my character. I checked with the flight attendants more than once to be sure of the time of my flight and the correct gate.

When I arrived back in Detroit, I had no money for parking. Luckily or providentially, it was the first day that they began accepting credit cards at this parking structure. I was blessed by my Guardian Angel. I arrived home safely just a few minutes before Gary returned from the G.M. Tech Center. Never did I tell him of my adventurous day! While I was hospitalized he found the vouchers for the tickets and figured it out.

We ate dinner and went to church at St. Lawrence as intended, as it was Ash Wednesday. I remember feeling sick after returning home. I lied down on the couch and fell asleep. Meanwhile Gary was packing for his 13th trip to China for his work with General Motors. Our son was in California with plans to return the following day from spring break.

In the morning, Gary said goodbye. I remember thinking I had a bad flu and physically felt lousy. He was upset with me when he left. Then things started to go downhill. Our dog, Wessley, got out and ran away. I got a call later from the pound that Wessley had been picked up and we needed to retrieve him within 48 hours, or he would be put up for adoption or euthanized. I didn't want to lose him, so as sick as I was, off I went to retrieve him. But I could not find the dog pound even though I'd been there before. I returned home, phoned them, and got better directions. Finally, I retrieved him. I arrived home without having a car accident.

Later I went out on my deck and my next-door neighbor saw me. I must have been acting peculiar, because he sent his wife, Debi, over to check on me. I said I was fine and that I was The Blessed Mother. Through the grace of God, we had told this young couple about my disease previously. Their next step was to call the police who came to the house. They asked me some questions, and I told them I was feeling sick and also that I was bipolar. Through our alarm system, they notified our emergency contact friends who came to my rescue. I remember either actually speaking in tongues or just gibberish. My friend kept telling me she could not understand me when I talked in that way. This was another sign of bipolar, specifically, religiosity.

In the meantime, Gary was en route to China. Shaun was to return from California where he spent spring break. He was expecting me to pick him up from the airport. Our friends arranged to have their son pick up Shaun from the airport.

Mary Ellen, Tom, and Paula, who each lived an hour or so away, were notified by my friends. They came to my aid. My doctor found a bed in a psych ward for me again. I was now hallucinating. I had been singing strangely and thought I was speaking in foreign tongues. My sisters, brother–in–law, and my son took me to the hospital. I was pretty much out of touch with reality when I arrived at South Macomb Hospital emergency room. I was then sedated. My sisters and Shaun took turns staying with me in the cubicle. Then I remember being seated in a safety belt in the back of a paramedics unit. I was transferred to St. John's Oakland Hospital psychiatric ward.

That was the beginning of a three to four week stay from Hell. I thought I'd never get better and eventually just die there. The same incompetent doctor who I had for years didn't have hospital privileges, so I was assigned another doctor who knew nothing about me. I was put on several different medications to bring me back to sanity.

Gary returned from China in a week as my doctor told him I wouldn't know him anyway. By this time, I was so livid at him for leaving me home sick and alone. My anger was so intense that I called a lawyer friend of mine, stated that I would need a divorce as soon as I got out of the hospital. He told me to call after I was discharged as he was aware of my illness.

People told me they visited me, but I don't have any recollection of their visits. This was one of my worst and serious manic episodes. I was forgetting simple tasks like how to take a shower. I called everyone in my address book to ask for prayers. By now, I had let go of the stigma of mental illness. I felt I was in the movie "One Flew over The Cuckoo's Nest." I attended group therapy and saw my assigned doctor about two times a week for a medication review and short consultation. I attended O.T. and participated in the various art projects that I could manage.

I do remember a pastoral staff member bringing Holy Communion to the floor. As soon as the bell rang for Holy Communion distribution, I was first in line. I always desired to receive Holy Communion whenever I was hospitalized. My faith sustained me during this and all my hospitalizations. It was a long road to recovery.

I gained thirty pounds in three weeks and kept having Gary bring me bigger clothes. When I was released, I did not even recognize myself in the mirror.

Just because you are discharged from the hospital does not mean you are totally well. My self-esteem was at an all-time low after every discharge. I sunk to the depths of despair. It felt like I was in a deep, dark hole. As hard as it was I turned to prayer. I would watch EWTN, a Catholic TV station daily. I said the rosary and learned the Divine Mercy Chaplet and would sit quietly in prayer much of the day. Slowly, I would come around, gain my complete sanity. Some confidence gradually returned.

Other Memories Related to my Life

THE STRONG FOUNDATION OF OUR MARRIAGE KEPT OUR relationship intact. We had attended a Marriage Encounter weekend in 1978 and again in 1997 to improve our communication skills. It is a faith-based, Christ-centered program for healthy marriages. It strengthened our relationship and our prayer life. We became active in our sharing group. We even took on leadership roles once my disease was under control. We had moved to a new home in 1997. We were invited by our next door neighbors, also involved in M.E., to join their sharing group. We've been involved ever since. We have made life-long friends. Another prayer of mine was answered.

Gary was my rock of support when I was in the hospital and Shaun was my reason for living. We never had a dysfunctional family life since I was hospitalized immediately when I became sick. I swore to never repeat the history of my childhood. Shaun would be allowed to visit me only when my behavior was appropriate.

Most friends and all of my family were supportive of me during these trials. However, a few good friends did turn their back on me and ended our relationship. The stigma of mental illness was extremely negative at that time.

During my recovery period at home, I spent much time in prayer and meditation. I allowed God to bathe me with his love. Without God in our lives, we could never have survived these 45 years together.

To this day, I can honestly say I am thankful for the cross God had me carry. Without it, my faith would not be as strong as it is today. I truly believe in miracles. One time, my doctor said, "You don't just have one guardian angel but a fleet of them!" I think she was correct.

God has used me to speak of my life's experiences on different occasions. At times I would share with acquaintances of my disease and discovered they also were bipolar. I was thankful to be humble enough to admit having this disease with others. We were supportive of each other and with some became great friends.

From age 25 to 45, when my mania was in check, I had periodic counseling that resolved my childhood issues. My life returned to normal. No amount of counseling, though, could have changed my chemical imbalance. I needed medication.

After such horrendous ordeals and hospitalizations, I decided in February of 2000 after my last hospitalization, it was time for a new psychiatrist. From the advice of my Christian family practice doctor, I found the doctor who has kept me hospital-free for the last 21 years. I've never been on Lithium again since it obviously did not control my disease, especially the manic episodes. My new doctor treats me with Zyprexa (an anti-psychotic drug) and Lamictal (a mood stabilizer). I have never been hospitalized since. The side effects of the Lithium did cause damage to my kidneys, however. The only sign of this disease is my bloodwork, but I do have stage four chronic kidney disease. I am under the care of a nephrologist to keep this disease in check.

From 2000 to 2008, I saw my doctor every four to six weeks for a medication review and an evaluation of my mental condition. Twice during that period, I felt that a manic episode was eminent. I had the fortitude to contact my doctor immediately. As he would increase my Zyprexa, the episode was controlled. Within 24 hours, I would be back to normal. Presently, in 2021, I see my doctor three times a year for medication review and to refill prescriptions.

I recall another significant faith-filled experience I'd like to share with you. It was years ago while Shaun was still in grade school. It was during a normal phase of my life. I had already turned my life and will over to the care of God. One day as I entered our first home, I felt a prompting by the Holy Spirit. I thought to myself, "What do you want now?!" I was urged to take a flower to the Basilica of The Shrine of the Little Flower in Royal Oak. I had never been there but knew of its general location. I paused but God insisted

He would protect me and I would be safe. In no way did I feel manic. I was oriented to time, place, and person. So off I went and followed His instructions along the way. As I made my way down Woodward Avenue I was told to stop at a florist and by a rose. I did not know where there were any florists. But He told me, all in my head, when to pull the car over to a parking place off the street. There was the tiniest flower shop. I went inside and there was a woman behind the counter talking to a customer. She looked up at me and said, "You want a rose." I was baffled. She charged me one single dollar of which was all the money I had in my wallet. I continued on to the church. The side door, which I attempted to enter, was unlocked. I entered cautiously. Upon walking into this huge church with many statues and side altars honoring many saints, a housekeeper walked up. "Would you like me to put the flower in a vase and put it on St. Therese's Altar?" Stunned, I could only say, "yes." After a few minutes spent in prayer before my confirmation saint's altar and her statue, I drove home safely. I kept this incident secret for many years for fear someone would think I was losing my mind once again. I knew for sure God was at work in my life.

I remember one incident that happened while in a hypo-manic state of mind. It could have been May, a Marian month. I decided to crown all of the Blessed Mother statues outside of various Catholic churches in the area. I went to an arts and craft store and bought silk flowers and the rest of the supplies to make these crowns. I drove to several churches seeking out Mary statues and proceeded to make a wreath for it and crown her. I did this without anyone seeing me in action. Religiosity is another symptom of hypo-mania, as is creativity.

Other times, I would go to charismatic prayer meetings to be prayed over. I would attend healing Masses and receive anointing after wards. I remember being slain in the Spirit at least three times. This same experience of having the Holy Spirit overcome me has taken place several times since I have been well, also.

One of the leaders of the prayer group made a comment to me that was quite upsetting. He said, "I think you are possessed by the devil." Shortly thereafter, when I saw him, I told him in no uncertain terms of my illness.

Once, I called the church several times to talk to the priest wanting spiritual guidance. I spoke to the young associate and asked for prayers. He said, "I will pray for you." I said, "I mean right now over the phone." Hesitantly, he agreed and did pray for me. I did seek counsel from a pastor once. He did listen to me, and was understanding and compassionate. I was just starting to become hypo-manic, if I recall correctly.

Another time, I did not feel well enough to go to church but asked Gary to speak to a different pastor on my behalf. Gary did as I asked. He told the priest that I wanted to talk to him for guidance. This priest was belligerent. He said he would put a restraining order out against me if I did not quit bothering him. As it turned out, this priest was defrocked for other improprieties a few years later. I was not surprised.

One evening when Gary wasn't home, I got it in my head that I wanted to go out to dinner. I called a couple of friends but no one was available. I thought, "What the heck, I can go by myself." I got dressed up and off I went to an exclusive restaurant in the Detroit area. I was seated in the middle of the dining room at a table. I felt pretty confident and courageous for going by myself. There was an older couple in a booth next to me. We struck up a conversation and before long, I asked if I could have a cigarette since she was smoking. I had a very nice dinner all by myself! When the bill came, I reached into my purse. I realized I hadn't brought my credit card when I changed purses. I about died. The waitress came to collect my payment. I had to tell her what had happened. The manager came over, decided they would keep my license until I came back to pay. I went home to relay my story to Gary. He was not too happy with me but went there to pay the bill.

At age 35, my husband and I were training for long-distance organized bike rides. Our goal was to ride from Lansing, MI. to Mackinac. The culmination was to cross the Mackinac Bridge. We rode 50, 60, 70, and 100-mile days to reach our 500-mile destination. By the time we completed our journey, my mood was starting to elevate. Vigorous exercise can stimulate a manic episode. That night we saw the aurora borealis. I was euphoric. It was magnificent since everything is more beautiful in this state of mind. By the time we returned home, I was in need of a psychiatric hospital again.

Another time, I drove to Alpena, Michigan and back in the same day. This is the city where I grew up. I had never before driven the whole way especially by myself. I didn't stay long because I did not even tell Gary I was going. I did many things in secret before I would get really sick. I was full of energy that day. I made sure though I was home before he returned from work.

One summer, my two teenage nieces came for a visit from out of state. We, including Shaun, drove to visit the kids' grandpa in Alpena. We stayed for a few days. By then, my dad was becoming suspicious of my mental health. He decided to drive us back home. We stopped along the way at a few tourist attractions. We visited the State Capital in Lansing. I remember being in awe of the architecture. It was a beauty of a building as I recall. Everything was enhanced during my hypo-manic state of mind.

When President Clinton and Vice President Gore were in office, I did something funny. I was not a Democrat, but I was impressed by Tipper Gore, Gore's wife. Her public stance was to erase the stigma of mental illness. I wrote her a letter and bought a wooden patriotic wall hanging. I went to UPS and sent it to 1600 Pennsylvania Ave., Washington, D.C. Shortly afterwards, I did receive a thank you letter from her. This was out-of-character of my normal personality and gives me a chuckle.

Since our desire from our dating days was to have four children, I was very sad to only have one living child. One day, I asked my female psychiatrist if I could go off my medicine to try to become pregnant. She agreed without hesitation. It was as if I were the doctor. I ran the show. Shortly thereafter, Gary saw my behavior was becoming erratic. He went with me to her office, but she did not tell him, nor make me tell him, my wish to conceive. She was quite incompetent. When I did think I was pregnant, I went to my PCP to have a pregnancy test. Of course, it was negative, much to my dismay. The doctor could see I was not completely normal but did not call Gary, my emergency contact. Later, I called him out on this. This was about the time I asked for a referral to my present psychiatrist.

Whenever I was hospitalized, I felt God's presence and that of the Blessed Mother and my own mother as well. One time, I remembered about the Miraculous Medal. I made Gary go out and purchase one for me. One thing I always did was to take my address book to each hospital. I would phone everyone and ask for prayers. I had to let go of the stigma that went along with the disease and ask God to intercede for me. My hospitalizations were far from pleasant; some were as long as a month. It was hard on my self-esteem. My confidence was shaky to begin with, always plummeting to zero during these episodes.

During one hospitalization at St. John's Hospital, I became close to one of the young, male medical assistants. He was always assigned to me when he was on duty for continuity of care. Needless to say, I related more easily to a male. As I was getting better, he revealed to me that I had "streaked." I came out of my room stark naked! I was appalled at my behavior but laughed at the thought of the reaction of the staff.

Another time, I recall being in a dining room with company. There were other patients with their visitors. I don't know what possessed me, but I stood up on the table and sang "Somewhere over the Rainbow," a favorite song of mine. Needless to say, I do not have a good voice. I'm sure everyone thought I was "loony tunes" but I surely enjoyed myself!

I only have had one true panic attack in my life. I was expecting my younger sister and her husband for dinner one day. While I was preparing the meal, I suddenly felt like my throat was closing up. I went to my neighbors and borrowed some Benadryl. l thought I may be having an allergic reaction to something. This did not help. I felt like I was going to die. I was definitely in a state of panic. When Gary arrived home, I had him take me to the ER. They assured me that my throat was not closing. I still felt that it was though. They gave me a breathing treatment. The nurses and doctors reassured me that I was going to be ok. They did not give me any medication. I was released after learning to do deep breathing exercises to control tension. We went home and I finished preparing dinner. When our company arrived, I was fine. No one would have known I had just experienced a traumatic event. I told myself that this would never happen to me again. The minute I would become in the least bit anxious, say in the grocery store, for example, I would breathe my way through the episode and it would pass.

On one occasion, I went for a massage at a different practitioner's office. He did not have a set fee but only charged what you could afford. I had no money with me, so I gave him some holy cards and was on my way. I thought nothing of this incident until later. I can't believe I was so bold!

Several years ago I heard that the owner of a prominent Detroit area furniture chain was building a house in Grosse Pointe overlooking Lake St. Clair. One day I took a ride down Lakeshore Drive. I found a mansion under construction that I figured was his. I drove through the open gate and parked in the circular drive as if it were my own house. I proceeded to walk up the steps, tried the door, which was surprisingly unlocked, and went inside. The great room was huge, beautifully furnished, with a wall of windows overlooking the lake. It was a spectacular view! Seconds later, a young man came into the room. He said, "You can't be here!" I turned around and left as fast as I could. Luckily, I did not get arrested for trespassing. It is a funny memory now.

Nursing School was another stressful period of my life. The instructors did not make it an environment to enjoy learning. I did better in theory than in clinical. I was quite shy. It was as if I were on pins and needles while working in the hospital. My first doctor could not believe I made it through such a difficult nursing program without getting sick. I did have times of depressions throughout those three years, however. My sister, Mary Ellen, lived only 45 minutes from my school. Once I had a car, I would go to her house and crash for the weekend on the couch. I would sob when Gary would leave me to go home after a weekend visit.

I worked at St. John Hospital in Detroit for about nine to ten years. Hospital work was quite stressful for me. I feared life and death situations. I prayed every day that no one would have cardiac arrest on my shift. Right out of nursing school at my first job, I cared for many elderly and cancer patients. Many times in that short period of time, I had to call family members during the night to advise them to come to the hospital. I grieved with them the loss of their loved ones. When I look back, I was just a child, 21-22 years old. It was a lot of responsibility. I became mature beyond my years during that short time of employment.

When I was hospitalized, my father would often come and babysit Shaun. He would stay with me during some of my recuperation period. Being the thoughtful person he was, he accompanied me, after being discharged, to each hospital with a huge box of chocolates for the staff. This was for taking good care of me. This was a bittersweet trip as I was not always treated kindly during my stays.

Once I remember researching ADHD, Attention Deficit Hyperactivity Disorder. I got it in my mind that this is what I had, not bipolar illness. I broached this subject with my incompetent doctor. She actually put me on Ritalin. This is a stimulant which nearly sent me back to the hospital. She finally convinced me that I indeed had bipolar and took me off of that drug. This was another time that she did just what I asked of her.

One time while I was hospitalized, I was diagnosed with hypothyroidism. I was put on a low dose of a drug named Synthroid after positive tests confirmed it. Sometime afterwards, I switched from my primary care doctor to a holistic doctor. She explained to me that the thyroid disease can cause mental illnesses. I researched that topic. I became convinced that this was causing my state of mind. My new psychiatrist squashed that idea quickly.

Throughout the years, I had become familiar with the St. Bonaventure Capuchin Monastery in Detroit. There was an article in one of the local newspapers that intrigued me. As my mother had had a healing through Fr. Solanus' intercession, I called there, spoke to a Brother who invited me to come there to relay my mother's story. Over the years, I had many meetings with Brother Ignatius, who was Fr. Solanus Casey's personal secretary while he was stationed in Detroit. He blessed me with the relic of the cross of Christ several times. This was the closest to having had a spiritual director that I have ever had. Our visits were special. I remember the last time I dropped by unannounced, he was too sick to see me. I had brought a dozen yellow roses for Fr. Solanus' grave but asked if they would give them to Brother Ignatius from me. The receptionist agreed to do that. He died shortly afterwards.

On another occasion when I was well, I went shopping to a local Sears store at the mall with Shaun. As I was perusing the racks of clothes, he joined a group of children watching T.V. next to the cash register. I lost all track of time. When I returned to the register everyone, including Shaun, was gone. My son was missing. I panicked. I called his name to no avail. I prayed for his safety. Then I turned around. I saw him walking towards me. He was upset at me for leaving him. I was upset at myself also. I was just very relieved he found his way back to the boy's department after walking to the entrance to the mall. We were both in tears. I could only imagine the fright the Blessed Mother and St. Joseph experienced when they lost Jesus on the way home from the temple.

Mary Ellen, who is just five years older than me, has always been a big support. She became a mother figure to me after Mom's death. I remember one hospitalization in Grosse Pointe when I was given a day pass. Although she lived a few hours away, she came and took me out to lunch shortly before I was discharged. We had a nice visit as I had regained most of my senses by that time. All throughout the years of my illness she was exceptionally supportive. She was, and still is, extremely sensitive to my moods. She could easily detect the days I was depressed by my voice on the telephone. Her comforting words, prayers and cards were gratefully appreciated. To this day, we talk weekly. We are not only sisters, but the best of friends. Over the years, I have been able to be there for her in times of need also.

Gary called Paula for help to admit me to the hospital another time. I had to go through the emergency room at St. John Hospital in Detroit. I was acting silly with the staff. It was embarrassing to both of them. I thought it was hysterical. It was kind of her to come to his aid.

I was in five different hospitals in ten years from ages 25 - 45 years of age. For the last 21 years, my illness has been under control. I have never been hospitalized since February of 2000.

Our Family Life

THROUGHOUT MY ADULT LIFE WHEN I WAS WELL, I ATTENDED all of Shaun's swim meets and other events of his at school. Between hospitalizations, I returned to my normal self.

I was a Eucharistic Minister and a home-bound minister of the Eucharist. I also distributed Holy Communion at a hospital and belonged to the Legion of Mary organization. We were greeters as a family at church. I even lectured at Mass for a while. I was the Baptism instructor for couples preparing to have their babies baptized. This included assisting the priest during the sacrament. For several years, Gary and I were involved in the pre-cana ministry for couples preparing for marriage.

Presently, we do home-bound ministry together, assist at soup kitchens, attend bible studies, play bocce ball, and participate in a euchre club. I love to read novels, too.

Since Gary travelled to China with his job at General Motors, we accrued many frequent flier miles. We travelled to many states including Florida, Maine, and South Carolina for many spring breaks. We've been to Arizona and hiked Zion and Bryce, visited the Grand Canyon, skied in Colorado, and toured California and all of the national parks and attractions along the famous coastline. Mt. Rushmore, Yellowstone, and the Grand Tetons are other places we've visited. We have also been to Hawaii, and Alaska. We travelled a lot when I was well, sometimes with Shaun, with other friends, or just the two of us.

We were able to vacation to Europe three times. We also went to the Holy Land. These were all pilgrimages. We experienced immersion in the waters at Lourdes, France and attended Mass at St. Catherine of Laboure's Chapel in Paris. St. Catherine was responsible for the creation of the Miraculous Medal. We also visited Notre Dame, St. Mt. Michel, a Benedictine Monastery, in France. We were privileged to attend a papal Mass with Pope Benedict at the Vatican and visited many notable places in Poland.

One time, I asked Shaun if I ruined his childhood. He responded, "No, Mom. You were like a rubber ball. You always bounced back quickly after you were sick." His answer made my heart swell with joy. I always tried to put on a happy face when he returned from school, no matter how I felt, so as to not repeat the childhood I endured.

I was also a more astute mother, having a good recollection of my own childhood. I recalled how much attention I yearned for. I needed positive affirmations. Looking back, I needed lots of physical affection, which I did not receive. All of these things I promised myself I would shower upon my son. I feel I certainly achieved this goal. My motto for living is the bible verse, Philippians 4:13, "I can do all things through Christ who strengthens me."

Since 2005, I've lost over fifty pounds, maintaining that goal weight. I can now be called "Little Margie" as I was nicknamed when an infant by a family friend, who happened to be our local parish priest. Even in college, I was called Lil' Margie, even though my weight fluctuated up and down and I was not always so little. The "other Margie" was tall and lean. I was embarrassed to be called that name.

Through a sound food plan, a strong prayer life, and support from family and friends, I feel emotionally grounded and secure. Each morning, we pray as a couple. I also have daily meditation, devotionals, and other prayers that I do alone.

The Serenity Prayer, "God grant me the serenity to accept the things I cannot change, the courage to change the things I can, and the wisdom to know the difference, Thy will, not mine be done," is always included in my morning routine. I often say it during the day when needed as well.

Emotionally, I have learned to respond to situations, rather than react to them. I am more composed. I try to think before I speak. I make amends quickly if I feel I have offended someone. All in all, my moods are more balanced and my disposition more calm. Sometimes I still need a filter on my mouth, though.

I must also give credit to another support group I attended for about six months, which helps people suffering with anxiety and depression. A friend suggested I try a meeting. It helped me control my thought processes and gain more emotional stability. I have learned many new coping mechanisms for the everyday trivial stressors that used to plague me with anxiety at different times. So, between my faith, my new doctor, great medications, attendance at support groups, involvement in our church with emphasis on Mass and the Eucharist, and my devotion to the Blessed Mother, I must say my mental health is in check today.

I thank God for all my family and friends who pray for me daily and have always supported me through each hospitalization, and during my periods of wellness. Hopefully, I strengthened some people's faith by asking for prayers. Through the grace of God, I never over-dosed or tried suicide.

We celebrated Christmas with my side of the family every year. These are joyous memories. On New Year's Eve, we again hosted a celebration for several years. This time, it was for our second family, our Marriage Encountered friends and their families. I always prepared a lasagna dinner for the event. We feel honored to be blessed with such a loving group of friends.

We pray for our continued health, for God's blessings for all and for peace in the world. We have been blessed with the fortitude and perseverance to endure all of life's hardships. We continue to believe God will sustain us through any challenges we may face.

Gary

I N THE OVERALL SCHEME OF THINGS, GARY SUFFERED AS MUCH IF not more than me throughout the years when I was ill. He had to witness his beloved love of his life go from a normal gentle, kind person into a crazy lunatic. Every time I got sick the same worries, fears, and sad feelings engulfed him. He was not sure I would ever regain my sanity. When I was hospitalized, I would soon lose all touch with reality.

He took mental abuse from me when he was trying to be supportive. One of our tell-tale signs that I was getting sick was when I would become belligerent, angry with him. I would antagonize him into a verbal confrontation.

It was unbearably painful for him to admit me to the hospital. First, he had to call my psychiatrist. Secondly, he had to wait for her to procure a bed in one of the local hospital psych wards. Then he would have to pack a suitcase of clothes for me, including all toiletries and quarters to do my wash. Then he had to coax me to make me go. I sometimes went without a fight because I still had the presence of mind that I was nearing the brink of insanity. Often we had to go through E.R. for admission. Then the departure from me for who knows how long. He never knew if it would be a week or two, or more. It was a devastating ordeal. Each time he felt sucker-punched. Every couple of years, ten times total in twenty years, the same scenario occurred. It was emotionally draining experience for him. I am sure he questioned God's part in this and also thought "Why us?"

During my hospitalizations he had to find someone to care for our son so he could still work. His mother and my father often filled that role. I am not even sure how he managed the whole situation because he has shared so little of his experience with me. He would rather not relive the past. It is too painful for him. He says, "You have been well for twenty years. Why do you want to rehash it all?"

The stigma of mental illness twenty to forty years ago was much greater than it is today. Every other person today it seems is diagnosed with anxiety disorder, depression, or bipolar illness. He had to deal with the embarrassment of my sickness with our peers, co-workers, and family who could not understand the disease. One time, his mother said to me the day after I was discharged, "I think you just like to be sick!" Gary stood up for me and proclaimed to her that it was an ILLNESS!

I am sure he cried when he was alone as he is an emotional, loving man. I could never have found a better husband. He stayed with me through good times and bad, in sickness and health just as we had stated in our wedding vows. Without him I would not be alive today. He never gave up on me… he persevered. We both suffered in different ways and different degrees. It was not easy for either of us, but it was always a horrendous experience for him. I have little memory of my hospital stays, whereas he remembers it all vividly. Those were the worst times of his life, which he would rather forget.

I can only imagine being in his shoes. It would have been a time of anguish to witness your loved one slip away into another persona. My heart aches for his grief. I can only empathize with him.

Over the years, he has shared very little of his experience with me. Only as I have begun writing my story has he shared little snippets of these dark times. He was originally dead-set against me writing my story but has since had a change of heart. I feel if I can give one person or one family hope of a positive outcome of this situation, one of my goals will be achieved. It is one of the most treatable mental illnesses, if the patient stays on the medication. However, many people get to a point of feeling good and think they don't need their medication anymore. Thank God, once I found the medications that controlled my manias, the side of the disease that caused me the hospitalizations, I never went off of them. I thank God in my daily gratitude list for my prescription drugs.

Our trials have strengthened our relationship. Our strong faith in God has helped our love flourish instead of wane. I have always heard that tragedy can either break a relationship or save it. We struggled with my illness for twenty years, from age 25 - 45. Thankfully, through God's grace and many prayers, our marriage survived and we will celebrate our 45th wedding anniversary October 9th, 2021!

Throughout the years that my illness plagued us, I always said when I recovered, "Gary was my saving grace, and Shaun was my reason for living." I am eternally grateful for God's hand in our lives.

2000-2020

GARY WAS MY NURSE DURING MY MANY MENTAL BREAKDOWNS over the years. From 2000 until 2020, I was able to help nurse him back to health as he went through a few different surgeries. The latest was June of 2020 when he was diagnosed with cancer of the prostate. Thanks to God and prayers from around the world, he is cancer-free. We cried when we received the report from his surgeon. We prayed prayers of thanksgiving while embracing and shedding tears of relief.

We certainly kept strong to our marriage vows. "In sickness and health, in good times and bad, for better or worse, for richer or poorer, and hopefully not for many years, till death do we part."

My bipolar disease is an illness I will always have. However, I don't let it define my life. I am first and foremost a beloved child of God, a Catholic Christian, spirit-filled woman, wife, and mother. I am a good sister, friend, and confidant to many people. Over the years, I have experienced what I consider to be miracles and blessings from God. Without the trials, I would not have had the many joys I received in my life. Gary and my faith lives have been strengthened. God has been good to me and my family. I am eternally grateful for His grace and mercy.

For those of you who may be searching for medications for yourself or a loved one or friend, I will share my medications with you. I take an antipsychotic to control the manias and a mood stabilizer to control depression. This regimen has worked for me for 21 years. Hopefully it will for the rest of my life.

In telling my story, I aspire to give hope to anyone and their families suffering from mental illness. Find a good psychiatrist who knows how to prescribe psychiatric medications. Many people rely on their primary care physician who is not trained for this job. I pray daily for all people plagued with the diseases of mental illness. The patron saint of nervous and mental disorders is St. Dymphna. May God give you the strength, courage, and fortitude to accept your illness. Stay on your medications, even if you feel normal. Without your medication, you are sure to relapse. Bipolar is a chemical imbalance of the brain chemistry. No amount of therapy can alleviate this disease. It is one of the mental illnesses that is treated successfully with medications, and I am living proof of that. I thank God for my mental health today.

Margaret Graham is a graduate of Hurley Medical Center School of Nursing and Health Enrichment center. She lives with her husband in Fraser, Michigan.

Her email address is:
grahammargaret132@gmail.com

Photo by Ray Marquis

Margaret. A. Graham